Blues, Jazz & Rock
Made Easy

WRITTEN BY TOM FLEMING

Amsco Publications
A Part of The **Music Sales Group**
New York/London/Paris/Sydney/Copenhagen/Berlin/Tokyo/Madrid

Cover photography by Peter Svarzbein, assisted by Greg Wilson
Models: Ethan Campbell, Canyon, Sonia De Los Santos,
Megan Leach, and Akil (Myself) Omari
Cover design by Josh Labouve

CD credits:
All guitars: Tom Fleming
Bass: Neil Williams
Drums: Brett Morgan
Recorded & mixed by Jonas Persson and John Rose

Project editor: David Bradley
Interior design and layout by Len Vogler

*Thanks to Heather Ramage for her understanding and patience,
and to Rick Cardinali for all the tea and cakes.*

Order No. AM 982344
International Standard Book Number: 0.8256.3454.7

Exclusive Distributors:
Music Sales Corporation
257 Park Avenue South, New York, NY 10010 USA
Music Sales Limited
8/9 Frith Street, London W1D 3JB England
Music Sales Pty. Limited
120 Rothschild Street, Rosebery, Sydney, NSW 2018, Australia

Printed in the United States of America by
Vicks Lithograph and Printing Corporation

Table of Contents

Hello. Hot in here, isn't it? I know: you're having a good look at this book in the music store before parting with your hard-earned cash. It's Saturday afternoon. There's a leather-clad *guitar shredder* with long hair and industrial-strength glasses trying out a *most* unpleasant-shaped guitar over in the corner. He's been in here every week since before the Flood, but nobody has ever seen him purchase so much as a set of strings. The staff, enjoying the weekly war of attrition, has turned up the volume on the TV set, pumping out the latest *Teach Yourself Psychedelic Urban Bluegrass Ukulele* video in the other corner.

"Excuse me, I'm looking for a bust of Beethoven."

"Er...sorry. We don't sell things like that. Try the gift shop around the corner."

"I don't mind if it's not Beethoven. I like Mozart, too. And Choppin'. And that fellow on TV. You know the one. He's got lovely teeth."

"I'm sorry, Madam..."

"Do you sell CDs then? Have you got Albinoni's *Cappuccino*? I do like that one. I can play it on the organ. Well, the first bit. It gets a bit hard after that."

Run away! Take me with you.

But wait. Something has changed. What's going on? The shredder has stopped trying to kill you using only sound. He's playing something really rather tasty. Actually, he's not bad, this guy. Where did he get *that* riff? Hang on, he's playing jazz now. Who would have thought he could do that? Is it even legal to play jazz out of uniform? And now he's holding everyone spellbound with a hard-driving blues almost worthy of Stevie Ray himself. You are having a strange day, aren't you?

What happened? Well, let's see. I'd say there are four main possibilities:

1. This is all a dream. *It's all in your head. Books don't talk.* You won't remember much about it when you wake up, which is a shame because the dialogue between the shop assistant and the batty woman was quite good, in a clichéd kind of way. Don't knock it, that stuff sells. If only you could come up with it during waking hours, you could earn millions writing lightweight comic novels and live on a yacht. Damn.

2. This is all a dream. It's all in *my* head. Let's not explore this one too much.

3. Someone cleverly gave the guitar shredder a copy of *Next Step Guitar: Blues, Jazz & Rock Made Easy*—yes, ladies and gentlemen, this very book! It's so full of useful nuggets, snippets, and distilled essence of musical wisdom that before he knew it he'd broadened his mind and become a well-rounded player in a surprisingly short time.

4. I'm making all of this nonsense up in order to sell more copies of this book. A remote possibility, but let's keep it in mind for the sake of completeness.

Buy this book and take it home. Now.

"What's with this guy? I know how to tune a guitar. Give me a break!"

OK, maybe you do. But, to my ears at least, a lot of players sound *very nearly but not quite* in tune. The difference may be tiny, but it does make a big difference.

Of course, occasionally there just isn't time. If you're playing a one-hour party set with little or no break between songs, you just have to "wing it." In this situation it helps to have a guitar that holds its tuning, and a good stage tuner.

If you're tuning by ear (and I often find that electronic tuners don't *quite* get there), there are several methods to choose from but, oddly enough, the one we all learn first is actually the best:

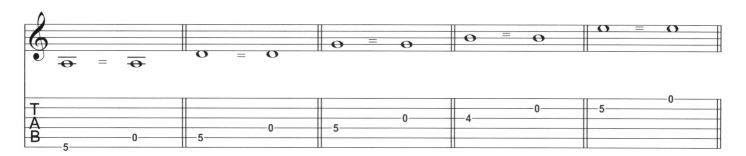

After this basic tuning, check the following octaves:

- high E string, 7th fret against open B string—adjust B string
- high E string, 3rd fret against open G string—adjust G string
- B string, 3rd fret against open D string—adjust D string

- G string, 2nd fret against open A string—adjust A string
- D string, 2nd fret against open E string—adjust E string
- top and bottom E strings—if they don't sound perfectly in tune, repeat this procedure until you find the error

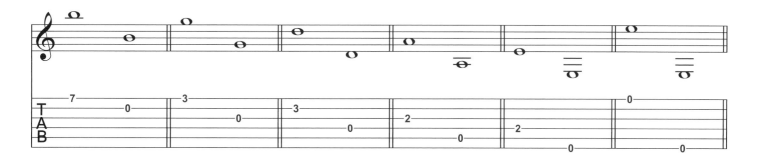

Don't be tempted to use harmonics. The modern guitar has to be tuned to *equal temperament*. Harmonics produce mathematically *pure* intervals, which actually sound better in their own right, but are unfortunately incompatible with the guitar's fret spacing.

For now, tune your guitar (from low to high) to **Track 1** on the accompanying CD.

Introducing the blues

Let's start our musical journey with a look at the 12-bar blues chord sequence. This forms the basis of at least a quarter of all the popular music ever recorded. In its simplest form, just three chords are needed: chords I, IV, and V. In the key of A (a very common blues key), this means the chords A, D, and E. These are generally played as *dominant 7th* chords—a key ingredient in the blues flavor—giving us A7, D7, and E7. Here they are in a few other keys:

	I	IV	V
Key of E:	E7	A7	B7
Key of G:	G7	C7	D7
Key of C:	C7	F7	G7
Key of D:	D7	G7	A7

The following pattern is *the* riff. Bear with me if you know it already. In one form or another, this is easily the most-played riff on any instrument, ever, bar none. Use it to accompany any blues-based song, at any tempo, straight or swung. We'll start in the key of A, as it's the easiest to play. In this form, we don't actually play the full chords, but the riff is so strong that the chord sounds are implied. You can, of course, try strumming any full shapes that you know for these chords, too. I've recorded it here as a medium blues/rock shuffle, but it will also work much slower or much faster!

Blues Boogie No. 1 CD tracks 2 & 3

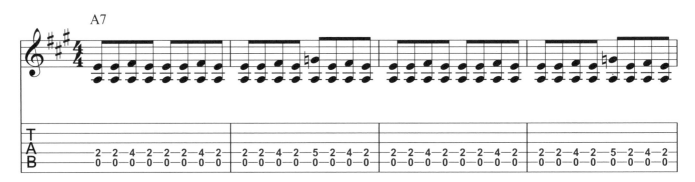

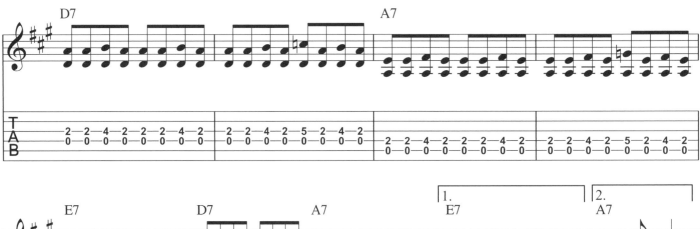

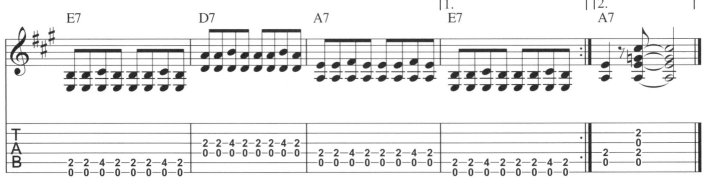

Playing the "Blues Boogie" pattern in any key other than A gets a bit trickier, as there's a little-finger stretch involved. On the plus side, you only need one chord shape:

G7

This is a bar chord based on the E7 shape. Barring at the third fret gives us a G7 as shown above; the C7 and D7 chords you'll need shortly are found at the eighth and tenth frets, respectively. As in the key of A, the full chords are generally not heard, but holding down the full chord anyway gives you the option to use it at any point, deliberately or accidentally!

The "rocking" motion of the pattern is achieved by adding the little finger to this shape:

G7

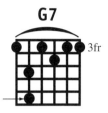
3fr

Hold down the basic shape, rock back and forth with the little finger, bring the seventh out by playing the three bottom strings together (as on beat 3 of bar 2 below), and you're on your way. Just remember to shift your hand up to the eighth fret for the C7 and to the tenth fret for the D7.

Blues Boogie No. 2 `CD tracks 4 & 5`

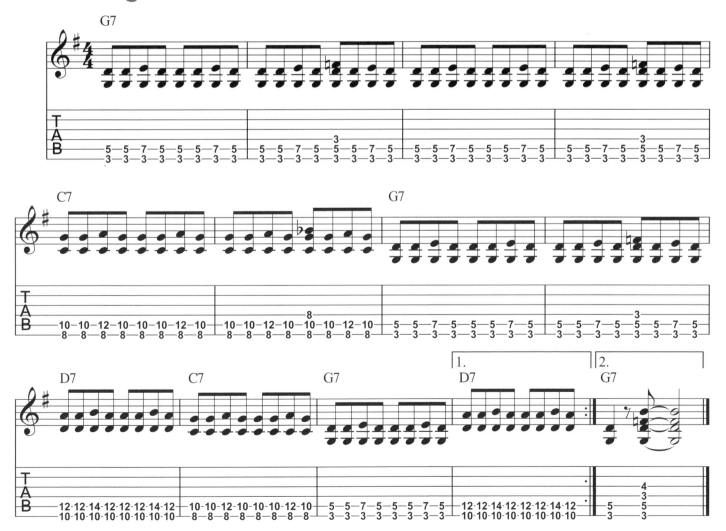

Before we look at some more involved blues pieces, let's get right to the heart of what makes a tune or solo *bluesy*.

The basic chord sequence of "Blues Boogie No. 1" (A, D, and E) was in the key of A major. In classical music, this would generally mean that the notes used in the tune would use the scale of A major. But using "bluesy" dominant 7th chords on I and IV (A7

and D7) introduces notes that don't strictly belong to A major: G natural and C natural. These notes are generally defined as the *blue notes* that give blues-based music its characteristic flavor.

Here's a simple exercise in bluesiness. Notice the sound produced when the C♮ in the melody clashes with the C♯ of the A7 chord, and when the G♮ in the melody clashes with the G♯ of the E7 chord.

Exercisin' the Blues CD tracks 6 & 7

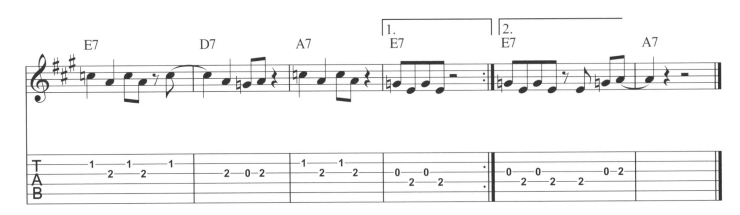

Combining these blue notes (the *flat third* and *flat seventh*) together with the roots of the I, IV, and V chords gives us a scale which is absolutely crucial to all sorts of music across the world. This is the

pentatonic scale, so called because it contains only five different notes. This is what pentatonics look like in the keys of A and C, for comparison:

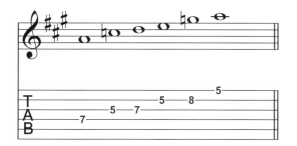 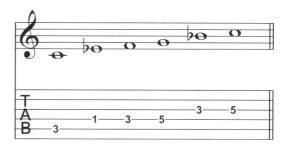

There's one more note I'd like to introduce at this point: the *flat fifth*. In the key of A, this note is E♭. Although not originally a blue note, this has become one—and our ears have become so accustomed to flat thirds and sevenths that it is in some ways the

bluesiest note of all. Try just holding an E♭ against any part of **Track 6** and you'll see what I mean.

Here's the "classic" blues scale shape in the key of A:

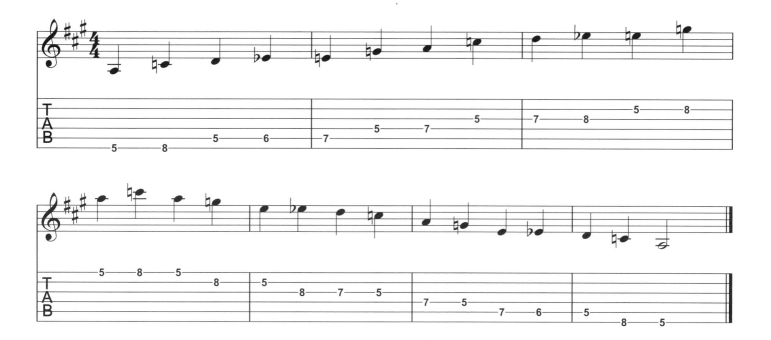

Get this shape under your fingers. Get to know it inside out, forwards and backwards.

Just as major scales and minor scales a minor third apart are related and share a key signature, so do pentatonic scales. The pentatonics we have looked

at so far have been *minor* pentatonics. The exact same set of notes can also be seen as a major pentatonic, if the key center is a minor third higher. Therefore the notes of the A minor pentatonic will also give C major pentatonic; C minor pentatonic will also give E♭ major pentatonic, and so on.

Although the minor pentatonic and blues scales can be used all over in a 12-bar blues, there are all sorts of other ways to add variety. One of these is to use the *major* pentatonic over the I7 chord (as it contains the *major* third of the key) and the *minor* pentatonic over the IV chord (as it contains the *minor* third in the key). To clarify this, look at our basic 12-bar blues in A. The A7 chord contains a C♯; the D7 chord contains a C♮. Using A major pentatonic over the A7 chord and A minor pentatonic over the D7 chord effectively *outlines* the chord sequence, rather than constantly clashing with it. This device is used by many of the great blues players, notably B.B. King and Eric Clapton.

Five of a Kind CD tracks 8 & 9

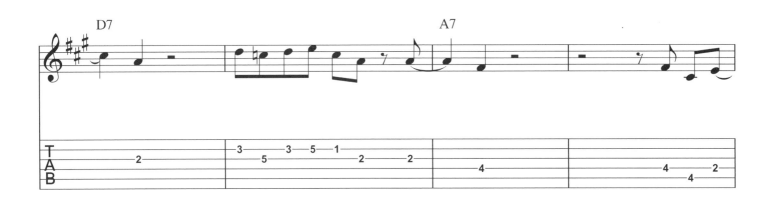

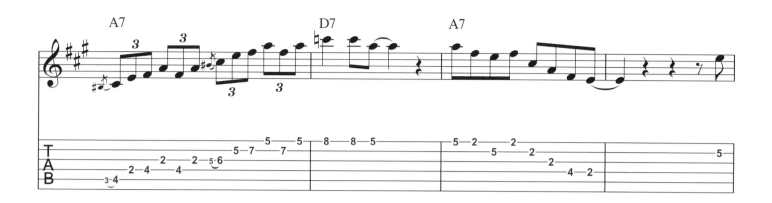

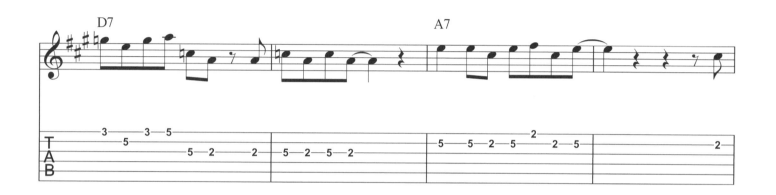

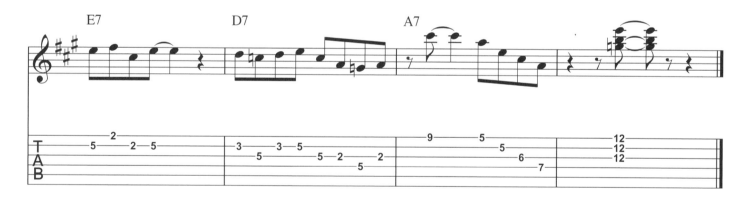

If you've absorbed these flavors, you're ready for our first really meaty blues solo. "Fat Man Blues" switches to the key of G and uses both major and minor pentatonics, as well as other ideas (see "Bends" on page 34). Most, but not all, of this solo is played around the twelfth fret. You can prepare by making sure you know the G major pentatonic and G blues scales in this position:

G Major Pentatonic

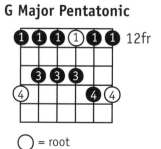

G Blues

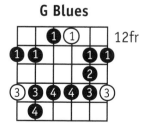

◯ = root

Fat Man Blues CD tracks 10 & 11

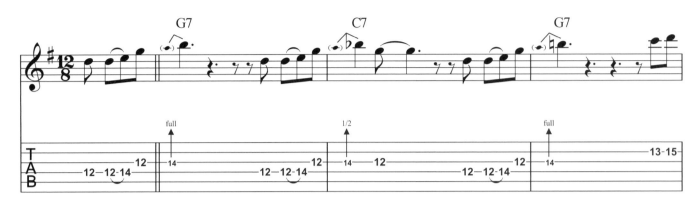

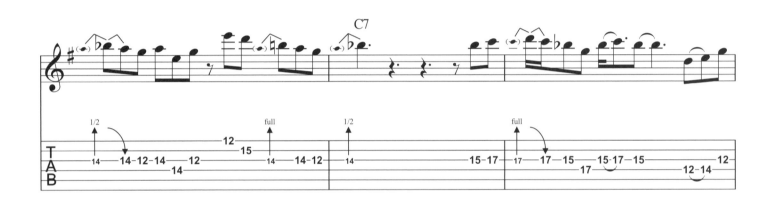

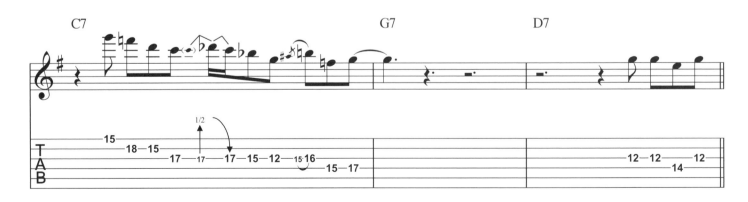

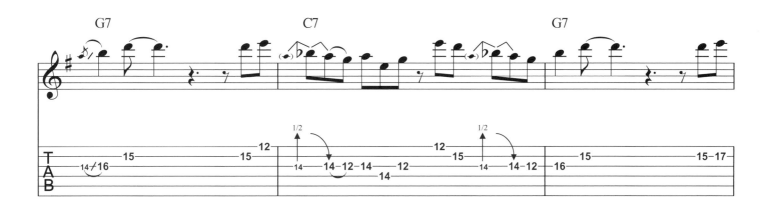

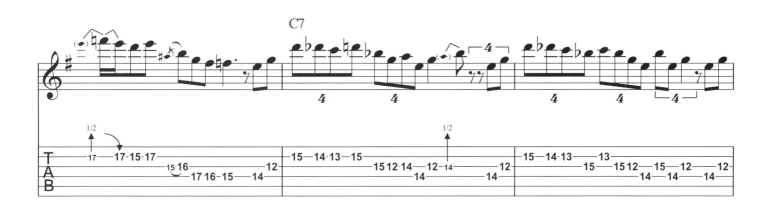

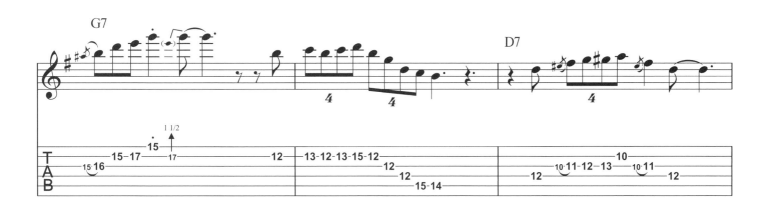

We're staying in G for the next blues piece. There's a lot of *double-stopping* in this piece: simply put, this means playing two notes at once. There are also many figures which I've written as a single line, but which involve holding a shape and letting the notes ring (the very first notes in bar 1, for example.) Listen to the demo and all should become clear.

There are some slightly tricky bits in this piece so I've put two versions on the CD: fast and slow, with backing tracks for each.

Chicago Blues CD tracks 12 & 13 (fast) CD tracks 14 & 15 (slow)

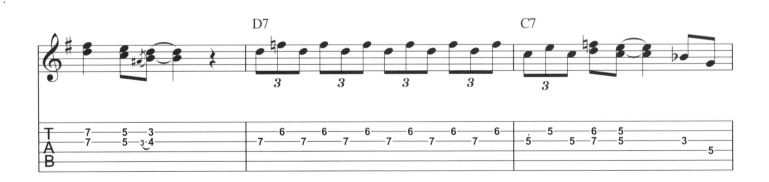

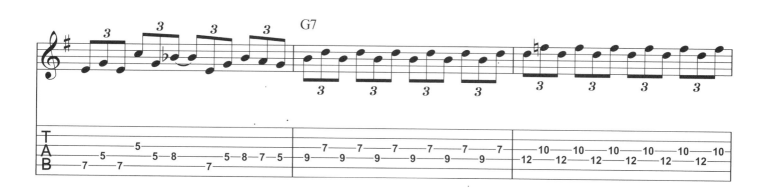

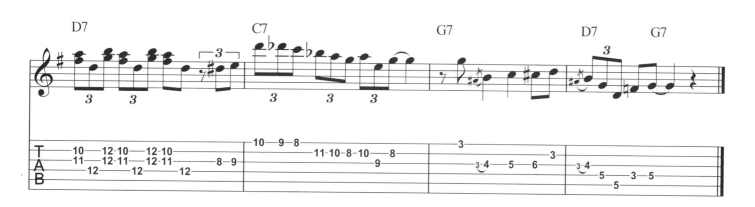

The final stop on our tour of blues styles owes a little to the style of the late, great Stevie Ray Vaughan. The main device in this piece is the *unison:* playing the same note on adjacent strings. This gives a punchy, ringy sound that is very easy to achieve and therefore enormously satisfying.

Again, the CD features a slow version to help you get the tricky bits under your fingers before attempting the fast version.

Bell 206B Blues CD tracks 16 & 17 (fast) CD tracks 18 & 19 (slow)

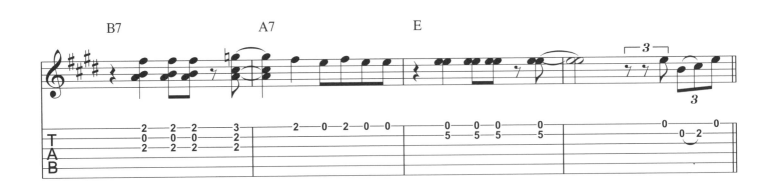

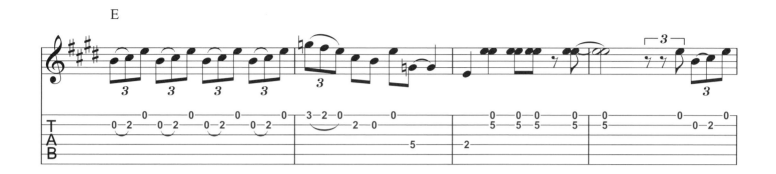

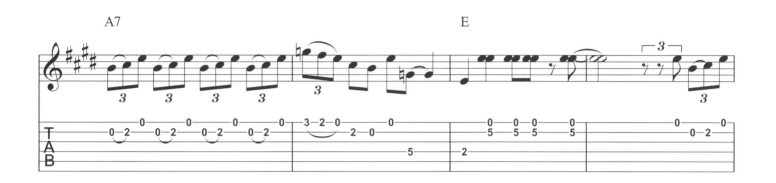

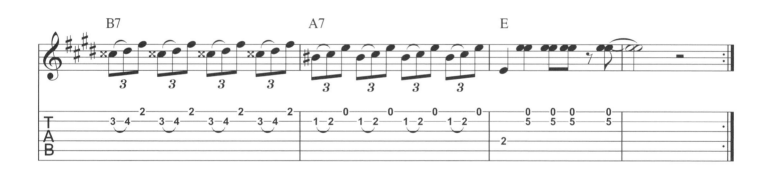

Modal jazz

Welcome to the crazy, crazy world of turtleneck sweaters and berets. Playing jazz can be a lifetime's study in itself, but my aim in this book is to give you a gentle introduction, equip you with some jazzy ideas to impress all those other people lurking in music shops on Saturday afternoons, and issue the obligatory warning that there's very little money in it...

I'm sure you've seen the terms "modes" and "modal" dotted around guitar magazines and other disreputable places. Much has been written and said about them, including an awful lot of rubbish. Here's my own quick contribution to the field...

Western classical music (from about the seventeenth century on) is based on the major-minor key system. That is to say, the scales we call major ("do, re, mi," etc.) and minor (slightly more complicated) conveniently describe the type of sound we are hearing, and furnish us with the the majority of notes needed to play any given piece. The simplest major key to demonstrate this is C major. This uses only the white keys on the piano (no sharps or flats) and the *key center* is the note C—this is the note that sounds like "home" when the music has come to rest. This is usually reinforced by the *tonic chord* (the C major triad).

But this family of notes can give rise to many other types of tonalities if the key center is *not* C. Playing white notes from D to D gives us a very different sound; this can be further reinforced with a new tonic chord: D minor. This is, in fact, the *Dorian mode*.

All of the white keys can act as key centers, and although the notes remain the same as the notes of C major, the sounds produced vary greatly. The scales formed from each of these notes are known as *modes,* and as you might expect, there are seven in all:

C - C: Ionian (now generally referred to as "major")
D - D: Dorian
E - E: Phrygian
F - F: Lydian
G - G: Mixolydian
A - A: Aeolian (also known as "natural minor")
B - B: Locrian

It is important to realize that each of these modes has a tonality of its own which has nothing to do with C major, other than sharing the same notes.

The modes were common musical currency during the Middle Ages, but fell out of use as classical music adopted the major/minor key system as standard. Modes only really resurfaced in the twentieth century, at the hands of jazz musicians, folk-influenced classical composers, and jazz-rock players such as Carlos Santana. In the modern context, any major scale can be used to generate modes: for example, the notes of E major (four sharps) give us E Ionian, F♯ Dorian, G♯ Phrygian, and so on.

The most important part of getting to know a mode is really *listening* to the flavor of that mode. The next piece uses the D Dorian mode. Notice that all the notes and the chords (Dm7 and G7) *could* belong to C major, but the Dm7 is so strongly emphasized that the piece is quite definitely Dorian.

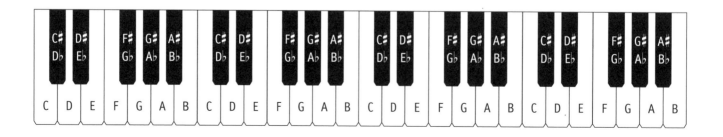

Dorian Daze `CD tracks 20 & 21`

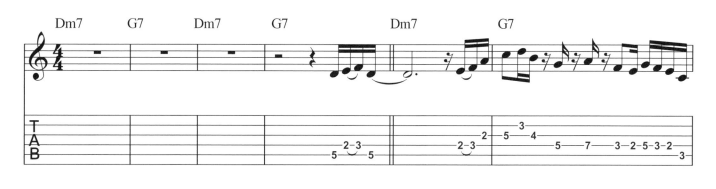

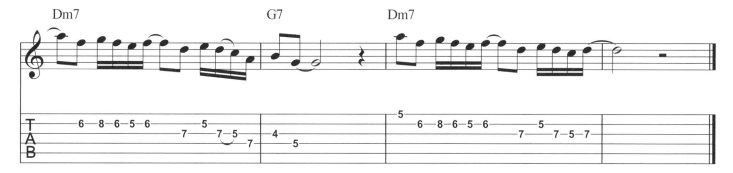

The Melodic Minor Scale

Changing just one note of the Dorian mode gives us another very important scale called the *melodic minor*. This can be thought of as a Dorian scale with a raised seventh or as a major scale with a lowered third. The melodic minor is an incredibly useful scale for jazz improvisation, particularly over dominant 7th chords. The theory behind all of this is endlessly fascinating and complicated, but for now I'm going to give you a very heavily simplified rule of thumb:

If a dominant 7th chord resolves to a chord a fourth above or fifth below (E7–A), use the melodic minor scale a half step above the

dominant chord (F melodic minor in this case). If the chord moves anywhere else, use the melodic minor scale a perfect fourth below the root of the dominant chord.

Notice in the next example that F9 uses C melodic minor (it does *not* resolve up a fourth or down a fifth), E7♯9 (which resolves to A7) uses F melodic minor, B♭7 uses F melodic minor, and A♭7 uses E♭ melodic minor. Mark Knopfler uses this sound a lot, and if it's good enough for him...

Smoky CD tracks 22 & 23

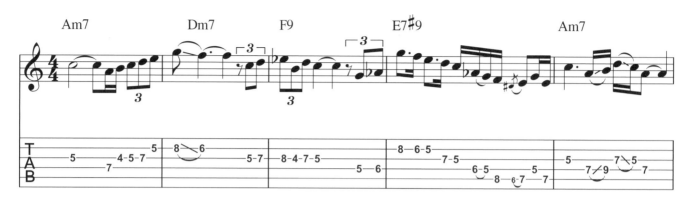

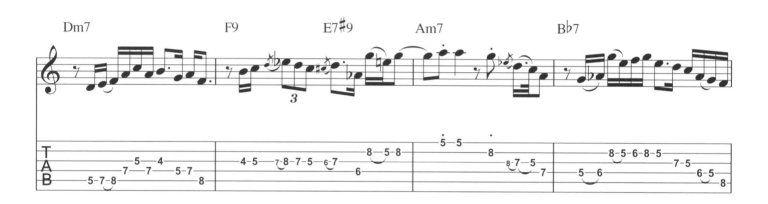

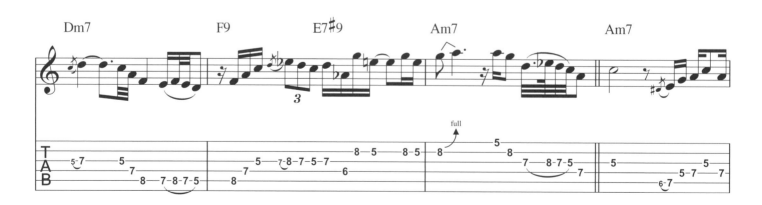

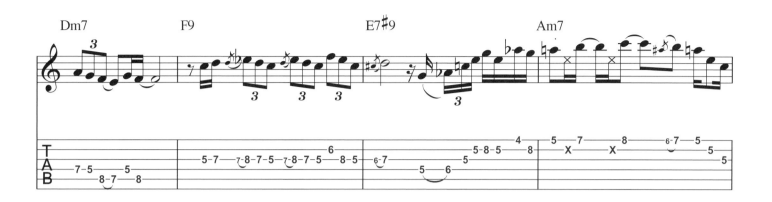

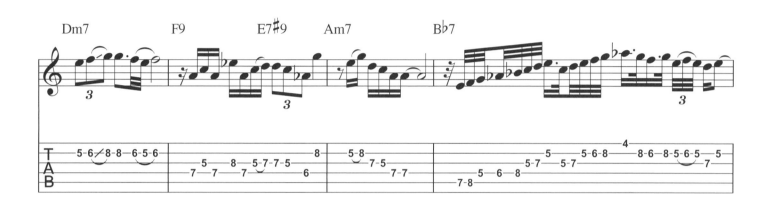

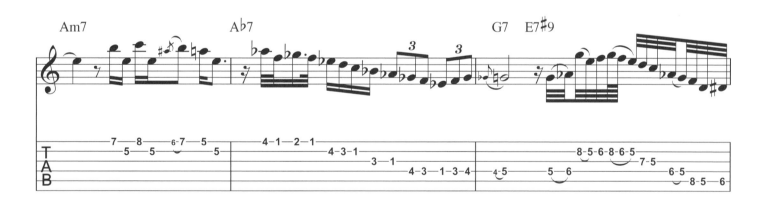

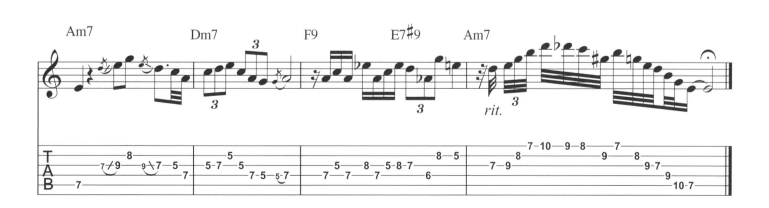

As we start to add more chords and temporary key centers, the theory behind jazz improvisation can get a little fierce. You can use a different mode for each chord, focusing on the chord tones as you go. For now, just think of it as modal jazz at a much faster rate.

Let's start with a bit of Daytime TV-style Latin smoothness as a warm-up:

It's All Latin to Me CD tracks 24 & 25

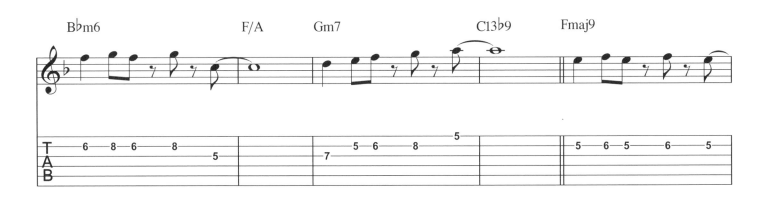

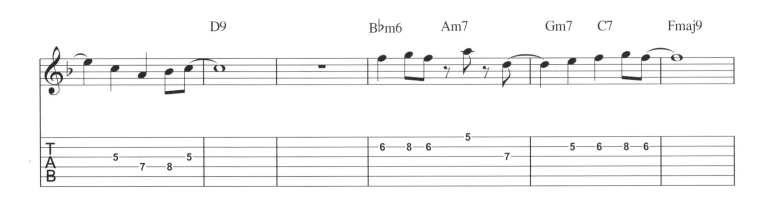

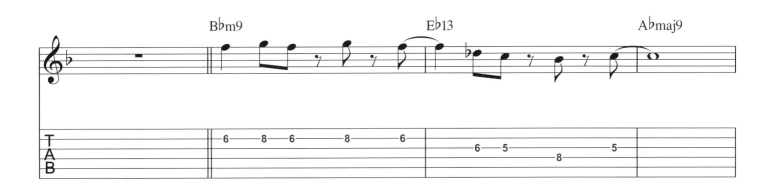

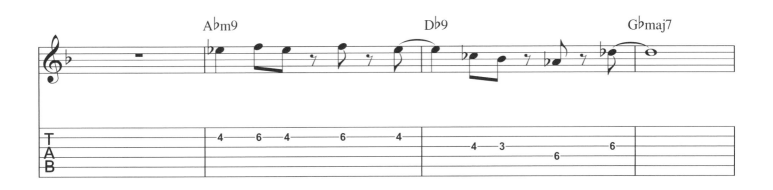

Octaves are just so *cool* that you simply must get this technique under your fingers. Playing in octaves is really just double-stopping using one fixed interval. There are only one or two practical shapes for playing octaves, and the shape only changes depending on which strings are used. Here are the shapes:

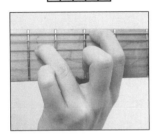

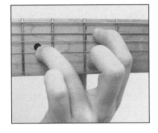

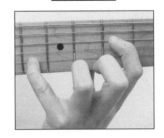

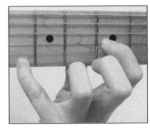

Lock your fingers in place and move the whole shape up or down as necessary. Mute the intervening string with the side of the left-hand finger playing the lower note (just the sort of technique a classical guitar teacher would disapprove of...but don't let that worry you!).

Here's a little ditty in the style of George Benson. There's nothing particularly taxing here, except, of course, the octaves in the middle section.

Blowin' CD tracks 26 & 27

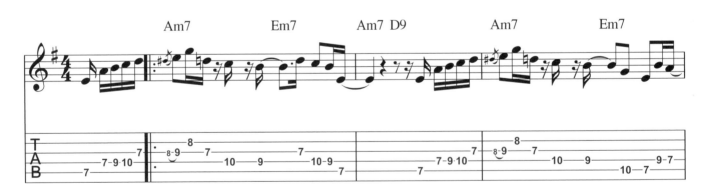

The blues is a key ingredient in jazz (and rock too, for that matter), so no tour of jazz guitar styles can be complete without a look at the *jazz blues*. Here's an "improvised" jazz blues solo. Can you spot the chord tones, modes, and blues scales? This may take a while to learn.

Blooze CD tracks 28 & 29

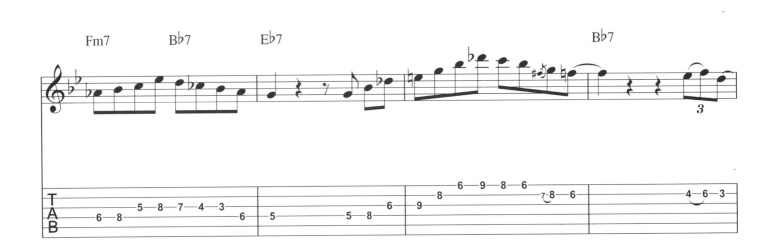

Are you ready for the big one? "Bop!" is an "improvised" solo in the bebop style using probably the most common chord sequence in jazz (after the blues, of course): *rhythm changes,* so called because the sequence is based on George Gershwin's pivotal "I Got Rhythm." Many other jazz classics have been written around this sequence, including "Anthropology" by Charlie Parker.

Again, there are two versions on the CD so you can limber up to the task using the slower version.

Bop! CD tracks 30 & 31 (fast) CD tracks 32 & 33 (slow)

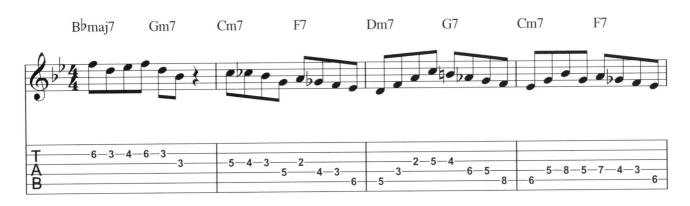

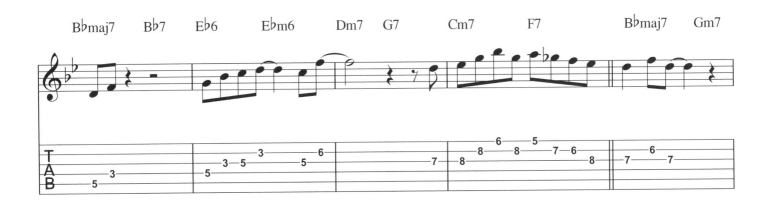

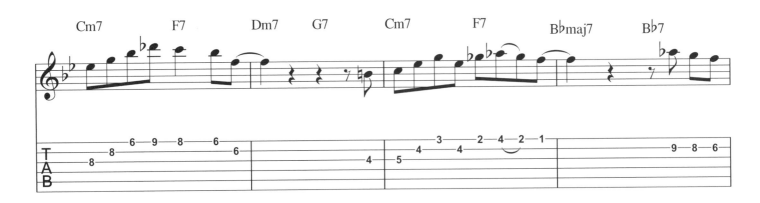

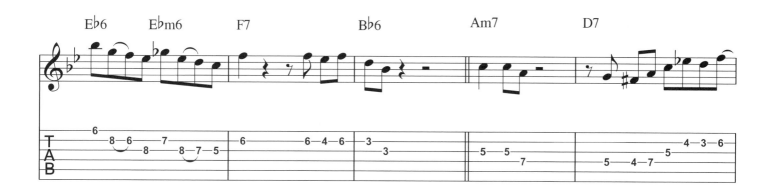

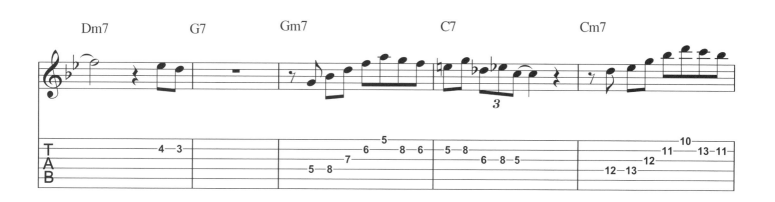

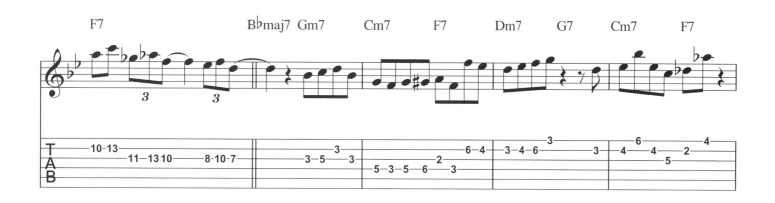

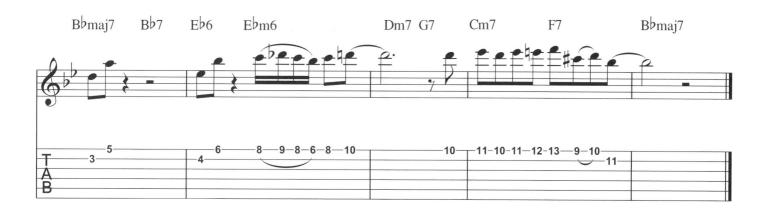

It's time to crank up the overdrive and delve into the leathery world of *rock*. There's no risk of running up against too much theory here. A great deal of rocking can be done using just ONE chord shape. That's right, the good old favorite root 'n' fifth *power chord:*

G5

C5

Hang on, that's two shapes. Well, it's the same shape, but it is commonly played with the root on either the sixth or fifth string. For that matter, open strings can be useful too:

E5

A5

So here it is, the purified elixir of all things rock...

Pure Power `CD tracks 34 & 35`

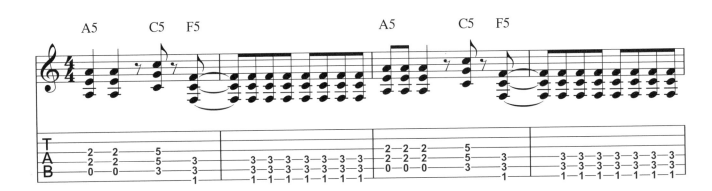

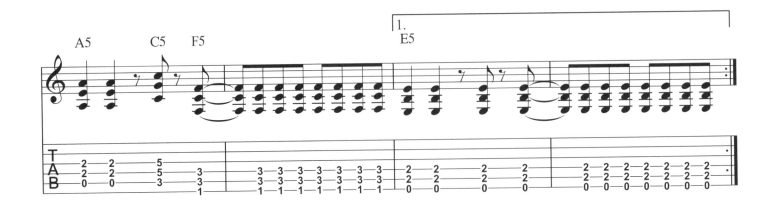

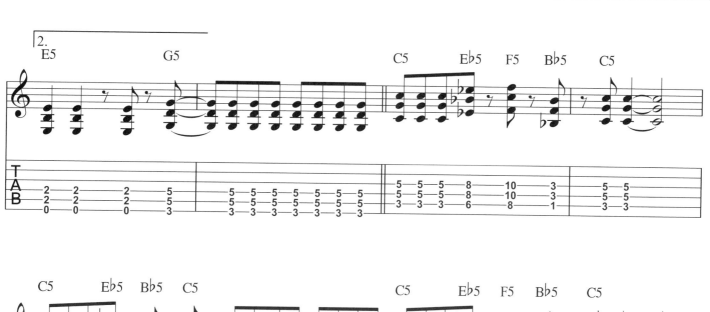

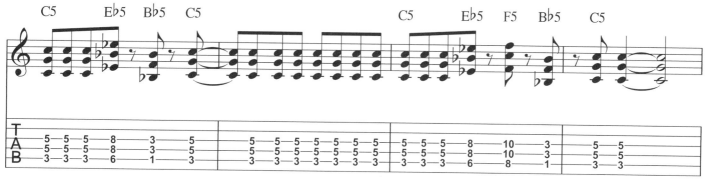

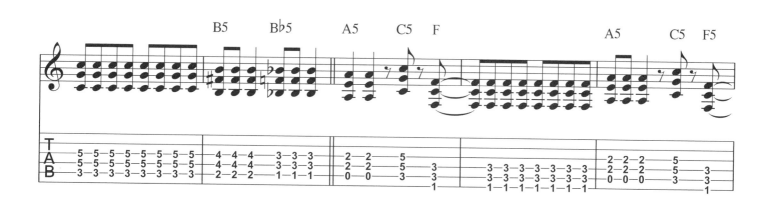

Power chords can be combined with a few other simple shapes to add color. Here's a little something to get you playing in a style somewhat influenced by AC/DC's Angus Young.

Steakhouse Rock CD tracks 36 & 37

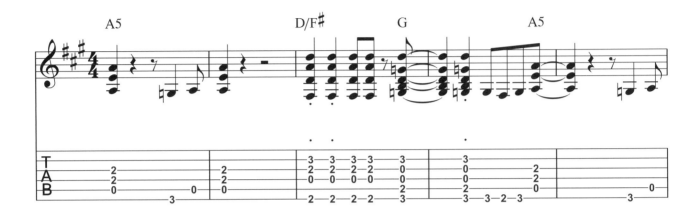

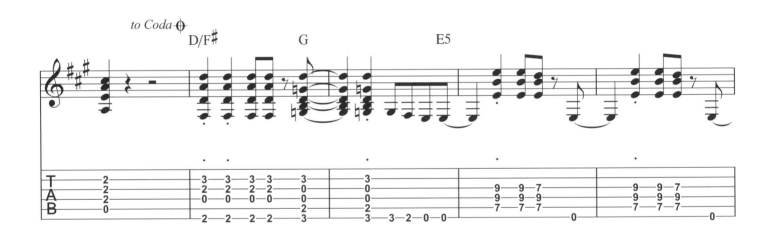

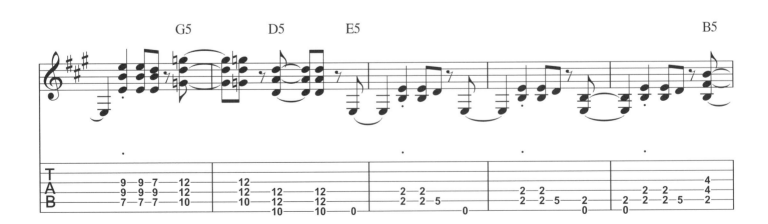

A lot of rock guitar playing relies on just a handful of simple but highly effective techniques.

Bends

No book on playing guitar would be complete without a look at this subject. String bending opens up a world of expression unique to the guitar. Most people find it easiest to bend with the third or fourth finger supported by one or more fingers behind it. Ultimately, you should be able to use your first and second fingers too. Bends are quite difficult at the first and second frets, but get easier as you move up the neck. Try it and you'll see why. The kind of bending I'm exploring here is generally "in tune," meaning that the note is bent to another note in the scale or key. With heavier gauge strings, such as those on an acoustic guitar, even a semi-tone bend can be difficult. Here are some of the possibilities:

Simple Bend

This is the easiest one. Play the first note and bend it up to reach the pitch of the second note. For most purposes, the second note should be perfectly in tune.

Bend and Release

Strike the first note, bend the string, hold it for the desired length of time, then release the bend so that the string returns to the original pitch.

Pre-Bend

This is harder. Bend the string first and then strike the note. It should be in tune already, which is the hard part. Getting good at this involves knowing your guitar well and *listening*.

Pre-Bend and Release

I think you can probably work this out!

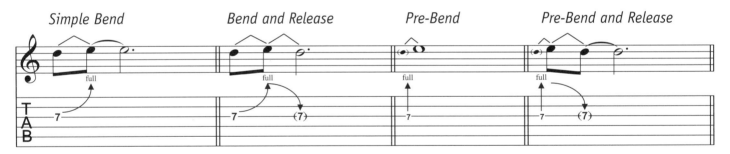

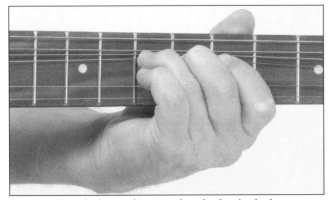

Bend the string to the desired pitch.

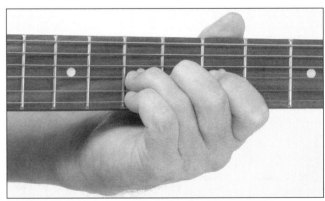

Release the bend.

Bend It Like Beck CD tracks 38 & 39

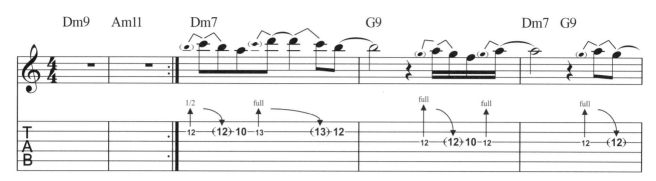

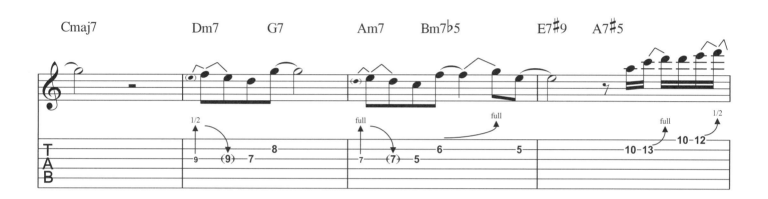

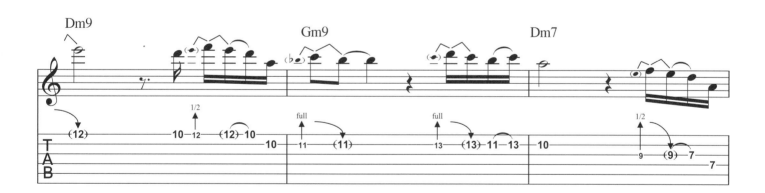

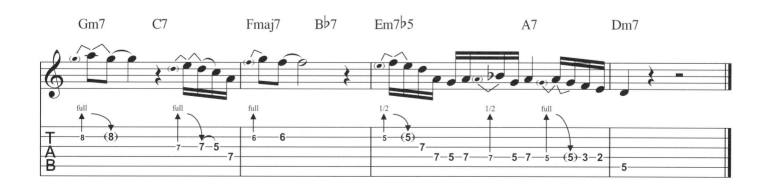

Unison Bend

This technique involves bending one note (usually up a whole tone) while playing the target note on another (usually adjacent) string. The two notes start a tone apart and end up in unison. This gives a far more powerful, gritty sound than simply bending one note. In this example, the note D (G string, seventh fret) is bent up a tone against an E (B string, fifth fret).

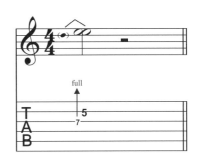

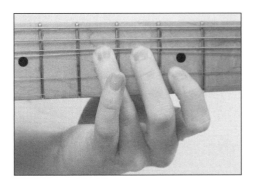

The next piece demonstrates this technique rather well, though I say so myself.

Rock It Up CD tracks 40 & 41

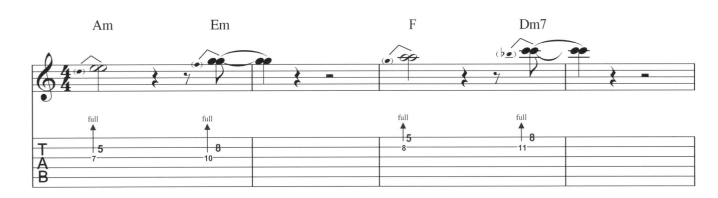

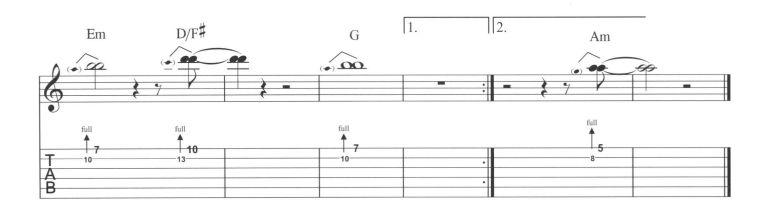

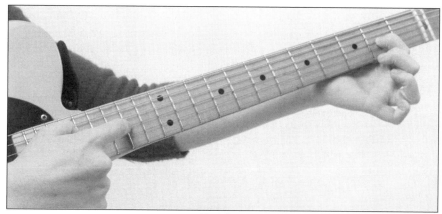

Tap it!

Right-Hand Tapping

Oh yes. No serious, or even flippant, look at rock guitar would be complete without mention of the favorite technique of many a Saturday afternoon music shop guitar shredder. Popularized by heavyweight rockers such as Eddie Van Halen, Yngwie Malmsteen, Nuno Bettencourt and Steve Stevens, mastery of this technique used to be the ultimate goal of every aspiring widdly guitar player. It seems (mercifully?) to have gone out of fashion in the last few years, along with guitar solos in general, but it remains an impressive trick. More importantly, it's great fun.

As its name suggests, this technique involves tapping (actually hammering on and pulling off) the fretboard with one or more right-hand fingers. Used together with left-hand hammer-ons and pull-offs, this can be used to play very fast and smooth arpeggios, pentatonics, and—although this can be tricky—scales. Here's a simple example with a blow-by-blow account of how it's done:

1. A right-hand finger (your choice) taps the high E string at the twelfth fret. The pick can either be placed between unused fingers, between the teeth, or on the floor. The important thing is to strike the string with the tip of the finger, with sufficient force to produce a note. This is not difficult, especially if heavy distortion is used. The left-hand index finger should already be in place at the fifth fret, because...

2. The right-hand finger pulls off, again with sufficient force to cause the resulting left-hand note to sound.

3. The fourth finger of the left hand hammers onto the eighth fret.

4. The left-hand fourth finger pulls off. The index finger should still be in place and ready for this.

Repeat many, many times, moving the fingers to produce other arpeggios as required.

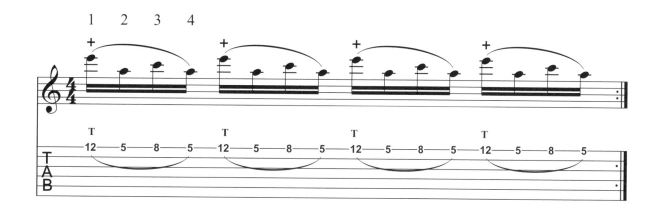

And now for the dreaded tapping workout. It's a short, powerful blast of pure rock excess. To help you get up to speed, there are five backing tracks, ranging from half speed (100 bpm) to full speed (200 bpm); I've also included demonstration tracks at the two outer tempos.

Tapping Exercise

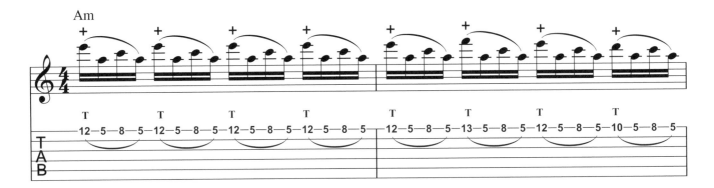

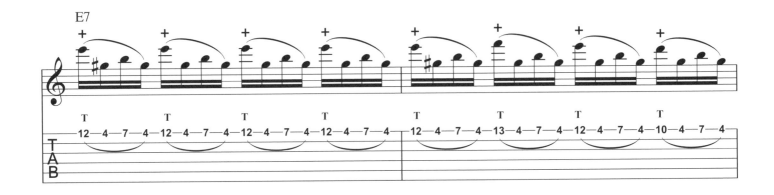

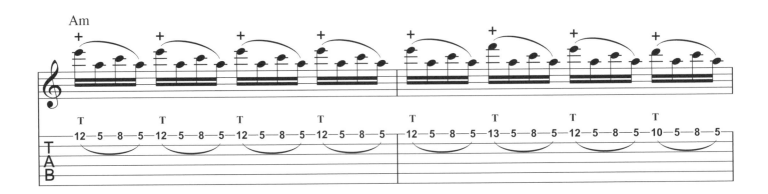

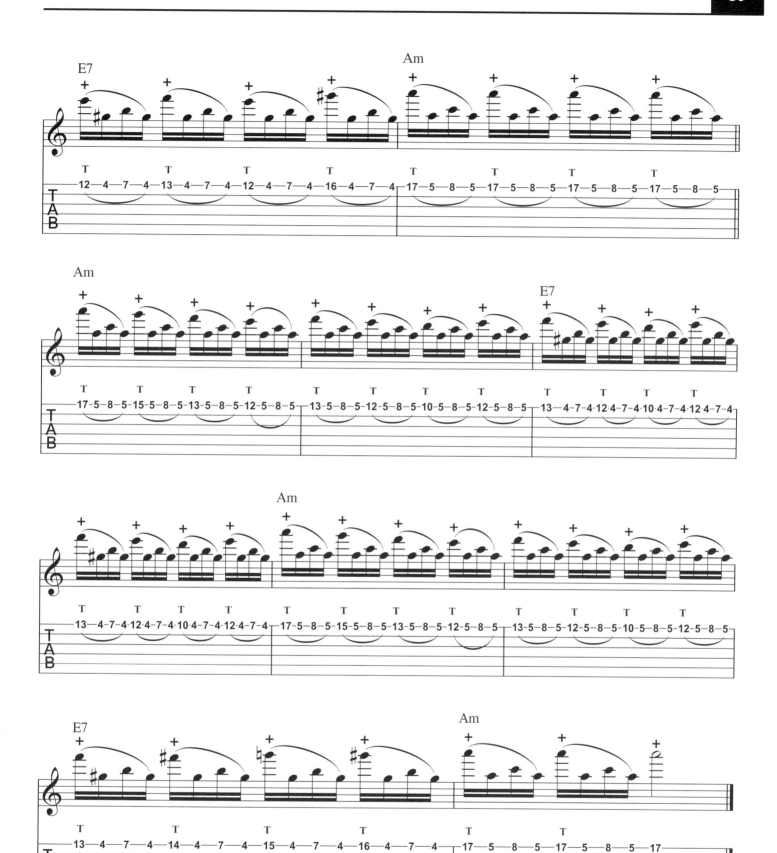

Bend, Tap, and Release

Here's a simple technique that will make you stand out from the crowd. Simply play a note, bend it up a tone (or semitone) and tap further up the string with your right hand. Remember, the tapped note will sound a tone (or semitone) higher than normal, because you've already bent the string. While you're holding the tapped note, you can apply vibrato (using the left hand is easiest) or release the bend.

Distortion helps to get maximum sustain out of this technique, but it works with a clean sound too.

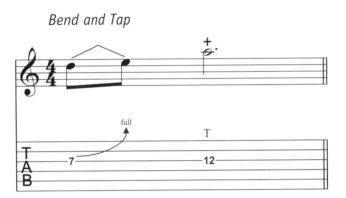

Bend and Tap

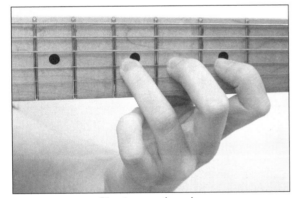

Start your bend...

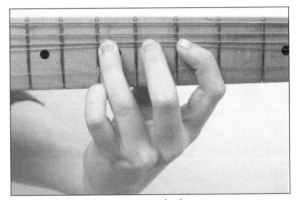

...up to pitch...

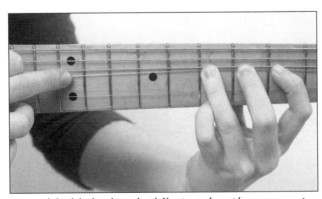

...and hold the bend while tapping the new note.

Bend, Tap, and Release

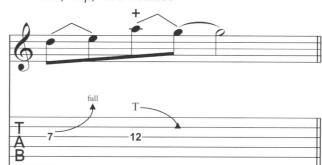

Hold the tap...

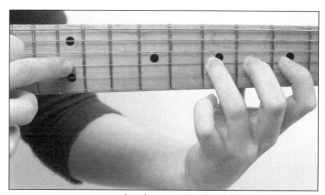

...and release the bend.

And here it is in action:

Bend It! Tap It! CD tracks 49 & 50

The "Neo-Classical" rock style depends heavily on one distinct scale, the *harmonic minor,* which is formed by raising the seventh step of the natural minor scale. In the key of A minor, this gives us a G♯. The interval between the lowered sixth and raised seventh (in this case, F–G♯) is called an *augmented second* and gives this scale its characteristic flavor, which is sometimes described as sounding "Spanish" or "Arabic." But, as the name implies, the harmonic minor scale forms the basis of Western minor-key harmony, too. Here it is in action, once again at two speeds. There are a few chromatic notes in here, too.

Muse-Ick CD tracks 51 & 52 (fast) CD tracks 53 & 54 (slow)

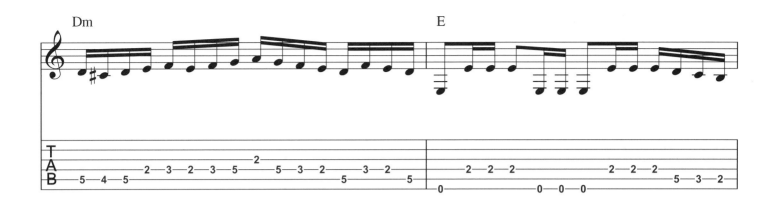

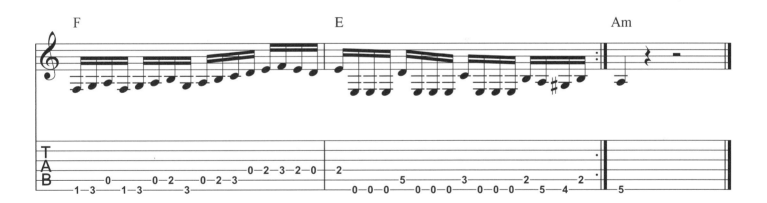

And here I must leave you. The paper has run out. I thought it would be fitting to make the grand finale a stadium-rock ballad solo in the lighter-waving tradition. There's nothing particularly tricky here; every note (OK, nearly every note) belongs to the key of E major. Go away and learn this all over the neck, the

way your mother told you to, and you'll be fine. You can, of course, use the backing track to play a melodic solo in E major of your own design. The choice is yours. Anyway, I hope I've managed to teach you a few things for your money's worth. Over and out.

Angel Wings `CD tracks 55 & 56`

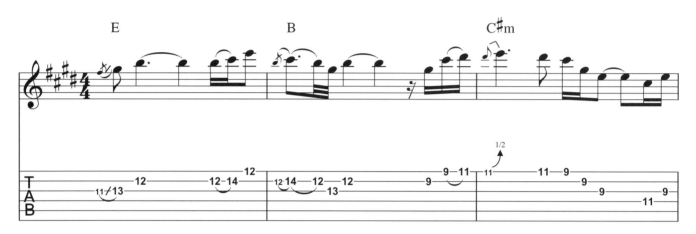

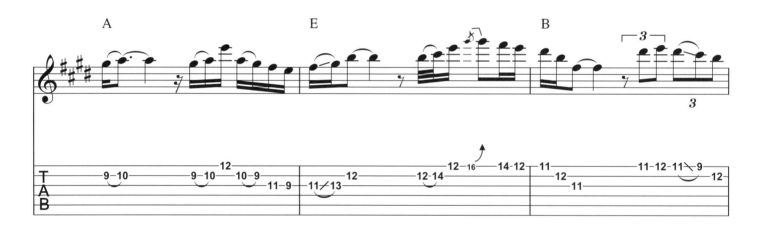

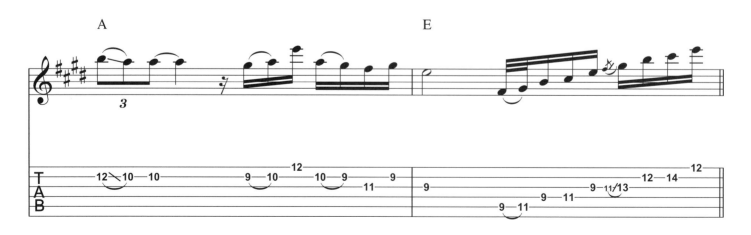

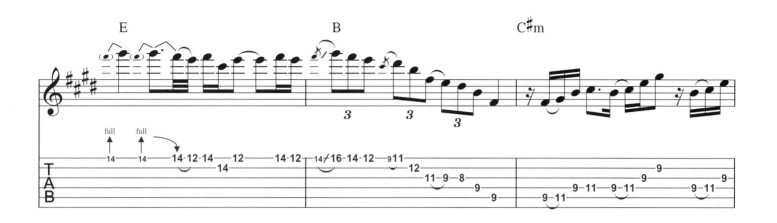

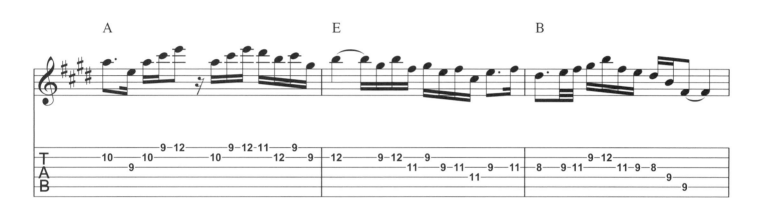

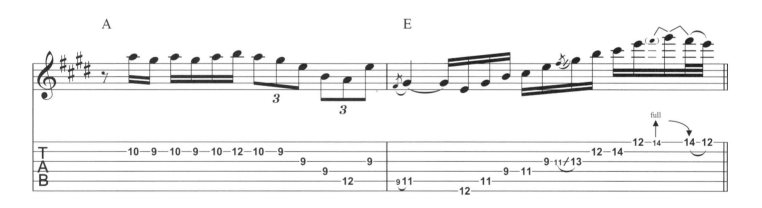

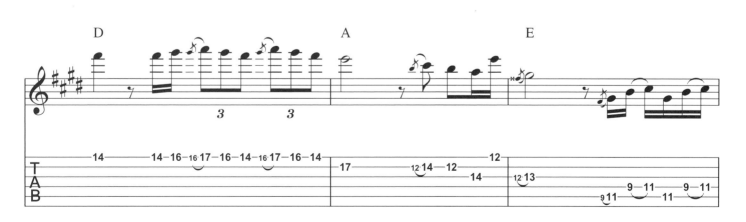

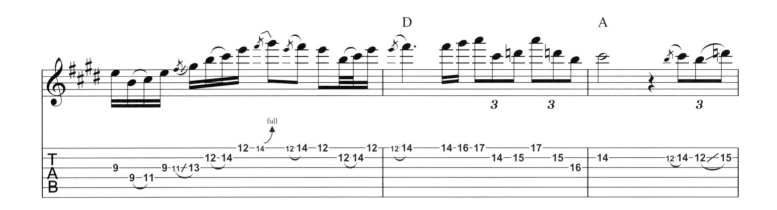

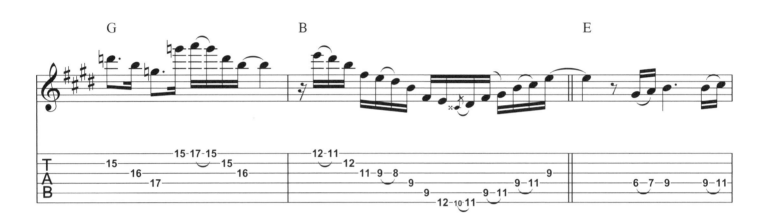

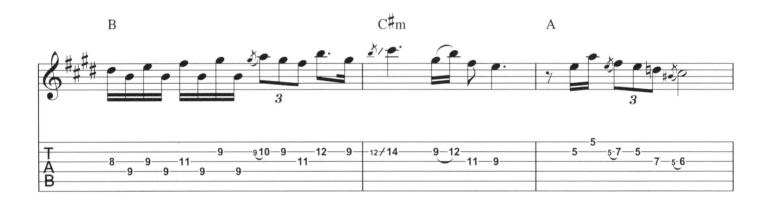

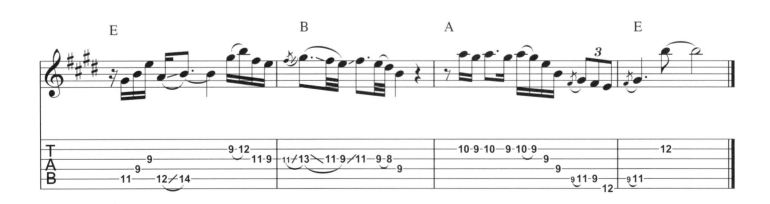

Suggested reading

Appleby, Amy. *Start Reading Music.* New York: Amsco 1992. A proven method to mastering sightreading basics. Whether you are an instrumentalist, singer, or composer, you can take a giant leap forward by learning to read music.

Appleby, Amy, and Peter Pickow. *The Guitarist's Handbook.* New York: Amsco 2002. Five guitar reference books in one handy volume: Guitar Owner's Manual, Music Theory For Guitarists, Guitar Scale Dictionary, Guitar Chord Dictionary, and Guitar Manuscript Paper. For both acoustic and electric guitarists.

The Complete Guitar Player Songbook, Omnibus Edition 2. New York: Amsco 2004. This compilation of three new Complete Guitar Player songbooks contains over 100 songs written by such great songwriters as Bob Dylan, Paul Simon, Elton John, Cat Stevens, John Denver, and many others. Full lyrics are given for each song.

Dineen, Joe, and Mark Bridges. *The Gig Bag Book of Guitar Complete.* New York: Amsco 2001. A sampler of The Gig Bag Book Of Scales, Arpeggios, and Tab Chords. Each two-page spread illustrates a scale with corresponding arpeggio and chords.

Every Musician's Handbook. New York: Amsco 1984. This pocket-sized resource covers rules of harmony, counterpoint, and orchestration. With sections on scales, keys, and chords, plus a musical term glossary.

Lozano, Ed. *Easy Blues Songbook.* New York: Amsco 1997. Learn the art of blues playing by jamming along to the actual tunes made famous by authentic blues artists. Fourteen tunes arranged for easy guitar with note-for-note transcriptions in standard notation and tablature.

Lozano, Ed, and Joe Dineen. *Mastering Modes For Guitar.* New York: Amsco 2002. This practical guide unlocks the mystery behind the construction and application of over 60 modes. Includes special sections on advanced and world scales. All of the examples are demonstrated on the accompanying CD.

Salvador, Sal. *Single String Studies For Guitar.* Miami: Belwin 1966. Simply the best book for alternate picking. A complete study of single string exercises designed to build technique and control.

Scharfglass, Matt. *The Gig Bag Book of Practical Pentatonics For All Guitarists.* New York: Amsco 2000. The ultimate compact reference book of pentatonic scales (five-note minor and major scales) and how to use them. Packed with over 400 riffs and examples; also includes a section on theory and more.

Scharfglass, Matt. *You Can Do It: Play Guitar Dammit!* New York: Amsco 2004. This proven method will have you spinning off chords, riffs, and solos in as little time as possible. Includes a specially designed CD with demonstrations of all the music examples plus additional backup tracks.

Willard, Jerry, editor and arranger. *Fifty Easy Classical Guitar Pieces.* New York: Amsco 2004. Contains a delightful repertory of pieces for the beginning or intermediate player, drawn from all periods of classical guitar literature. Includes a full-length CD of all the pieces performed by the author. Learn pieces by Sor, Carulli, Giuliani, Dowland, Bach, DeVisee, and many more.